Henry Koplik

Urogenital Blenorrhoea in Children

Henry Koplik

Urogenital Blenorrhoea in Children

ISBN/EAN: 9783337816384

Printed in Europe, USA, Canada, Australia, Japan

Cover: Foto ©Andreas Hilbeck / pixelio.de

More available books at **www.hansebooks.com**

UROGENITAL BLENORRHŒA IN CHILDREN.[1]

VULVO-VAGINITIS IN GIRLS—URETHRITIS IN BOYS.

A Clinical and Bacteriological Study.

BY

HENRY KOPLIK, M.D.,

New York.

CLASSIFICATION and Symptomatology.—Specific gonor-rhœal inflammation of the genital tract in young children, girls and boys, has of late become the subject of renewed study. It has been pointedly shown in most recent bro-chures, Epstein and Cahen-Brach, that the condition seen so often in large clinics in young girls and boys, is really a gonorrhœal one, and should be treated from that stand-point. The data upon which such conclusions are based, are identical with those which are brought to bear upon the diagno-sis of urethral or vaginal discharge in the adult. The publi-cations of Pott, von Dusch, Spaeth, which first placed the so-called vulvo-vaginitis of small children and young girls among the gonorrhœal affections naturally met with a degree of silent opposition. It may, in the writer's experience, be classed among the common affections of childhood. The cases which are recorded in this paper, are by no means the experience of the author, but they are simply the experience of the last six months. They record the cases as they come in rotation, and give a good picture of what we may learn from a study of this affection. During the past six years the writer has seen more than two hundred mixed blenorrhœas of the genitals (girls and boys) in children. The present paper will include some inter-esting data on contagion. All the authors who thus far have studied this affection have, with the brilliant exception of Ep-stein, failed to acquaint themselves with the conditions, sympto-matic and bacteriological, present in the normal vagina and urethra of children who were not suffering from abnormal dis-charges. It certainly bears directly upon the understanding of the specific catarrh, and justifies a classification of urogenital blenorrhœas, which will be adopted in this paper. Epstein has shown that in the new-born infant there is a discharge which is anatomically and physiologically normal, an

---

[1] The title " urogenital blenorrhœa " has been adopted as proposed by Cahen-Brach be-ing more elegant and correct anatomically than the old term of vulvo-vaginitis.

adhesive discharge from the vagina, consisting of epithelial cells, and micro-organisms. The introitus vaginæ in these children is not reddened, swollen, or in any way inflamed. In a few days after birth this normal discharge may become yellow, or even (in icterus) icteric. If we examine such discharge we find no leucocytes. After two weeks the rose color of the mucous membrane is restored, and the discharge ceases. This he has called desquammative catarrh of the new-born. It is a physiological process. Epstein mentions a simple catarrhal condition of the new-born urogenital tract, and cases of true gonorrhœa of the same tract. Epstein's material being an immense number of new-born children only, he has not described conditions of later child-life. The author of this paper wishes *first*, to describe a peculiar condition of the urethra and vagina in very young female children. The mothers come to the physician and relate that the child complains of pain upon urination or will cry when passing urine. Here examination will reveal a reddened introitus somewhat swollen and exceedingly tender, a few red points, apparently erosious, appear around the hymen and the urethral orifice. This condition is combined with a very slight serous discharge. The surface may be bathed with it or even the labia majora may be moist. This is a peculiar condition, simple in its nature, not, I think, the result of any unnatural interference. Uncleanliness, lithiasis, the adherence of smegma or dusting powders may cause this condition. It is really a primary catarrhal stage, and rarely presents much yellow secretion. It disappears as soon as rationally understood and treated. A *second group* of cases in young girls are the simple catarrhal cases. These children suffer from a scanty or profuse, purulent discharge from the vulva. It may, on examination, be seen to bathe the introitus. It comes from the urethra and vagina, and presents all the features clinically of the next group, but is of an innocent, non-specific nature, though infectious. The *third group* of cases in young girls and babies are the true gonorrhœas. In this set of cases we are confronted with a profuse, yellow or greenish yellow, adhesive, or thin discharge from the urethra and vagina. There is swelling of the mucous membrane, and the urethral opening is bathed in pus, which flows down over the hymenal opening and escapes with the vaginal discharge from the vulva, and dries in crusts upon the labia majora.

The *simple catarrh* of the urethra and *vagina* in children and young girls is not so infrequent, and will be found to present as

stated above, symptoms and physical signs which may con-
found it with the true gonorrhœal discharges. The urethral
opening is swollen and inflamed, the hymenal orifice, the
fringe of mucous membrane, is also swollen and very sensitive
to the touch. The discharge appears to have the same physical
characteristics as the true gonorrhœal cases. It is yellow, thin,
greenish or thick and viscid or milky in hue. There is a tendency of such pus to dry on the labia majora, and the whole
picture tells of severe local disturbance. The pus examined
shows, however, the true nature of this affection. It takes but
careful examination to see that microscopically the discharge
in these cases is not gonorrhœal. We have desquammated
epithelium and leucocytes, bacteria, such forms as rods, cocci
and diplococci. These rods, cocci and diplococci may exist in
leucocytes, they may also exist upon epithelium cells, but the
leucocyte to which our study in this disease is chiefly directed
shows in its cell substance a mass of bacteria, we find rods,
cocci and diplococci in the same leucocyte. Leucocytes exist,
showing isolated diplococci, but with all this we find none of the
bacteriological peculiarities common to a specific gonorrhœal
discharge of the adult male. The history of such discharges
are almost identical with that of the specific gonorrhœal one.
A peculiar persistence even with careful treatment, at most a
diminution and improvement but still the baffling continuance
of the disease which lasts almost the same length of time as the
gonorrhœal forms. Treatment may diminish as stated, the
discharge, and the peculiar anatomical structure of the parts in
the female make this matter easy to understand. I know that
in the male adult a non-specific urethral discharge is a rarity,
but this does not invalidate the daily experience that in infants
and young girls an infectious non-specific discharge is not infrequent. There is in some cases pain upon urination, a
frequent desire to micturate, and in one case at least, I have
seen the discharge complicated with inguinal bubo. In the
non-specific discharge erosions of the introitus also are present,
but the appearances in the vagina itself are none the less inter-
esting. Here in the cases I have been able to examine by means
of a male urethral speculum it will be seen that the mucous
membrane in its folds and rugæ contains a purulent discharge;
the cases I have examined did not show erosions in the
vagina. The collum uteri was a more pinkish red than the
vagina and in the cervix a drop of pus was distinctly visible.
The cervix of the uterus itself is therefore the seat of

disease in many cases. We can thus understand how difficult is the treatment and therapeutic disposition of these cases. (Spaeth and Cahen-Brach also Bumm report like appearances.) The many folds of the vagina, the thousands of minute asperities of the cervix uteri all contain myriads of micro-organisms which cannot be reached by our agencies. The urethra which has, I think, erroneously been selected as the point of attack in all varieties of vulvo-vaginitis may be said to have a species of constant natural irrigation through the passage of the stream of urine over the canal. The tendency is therefore in the direction of cleanliness of this simple tube in female children. The vagina and cervix, the small, undeveloped crypts in the same and also the undeveloped crypts (Bartolini ducts) of the introitus all being infected in the simple as well as the gonorrhœal blenorrhœa tend to prolong the disease in both forms, however the simple catarrhal form of vulvo vaginitis is infectious; by this I mean it may be communicated from child to child. I have seen this in two sisters who slept together and where repeated examination failed to show anything specific of gonorrhœa. The non-specific form may last for months, they may apparently cease and then recur in greater or less severity. I doubt whether any one to-day believes in the scrofulous or marasmic theories regarding these affections, but they may be favored by bad surroundings which invite a definite infection. The methods of infection will be treated of later.

True Gonorrhœas.—The next group into which the cases of blenorrhœa of the urethra and vagina divide themselves is the true gonorrhœa of these parts. Pott, von Dusch, Spaeth, Steinschneider have all described these cases, and lately, Epstein has described gonorrhœa in new-born female infants, and lastly, Cahen-Brach has collated some thirty cases of the disease. In these cases it is most difficult to trace the origin of the disease, which at times becomes epidemic and seems to affect masses of children (Fraenkel). The authors who have busied themselves studying the affection have, with reluctance, some of them admitted the gonorrhœal nature of the affection. The little patients are brought to the physician with the history that the only thing noticed wrong with the child was a discharge from the vulva. All other history is obtained, in girls especially, with the greatest difficulty . Examination reveals a thick yellow, or greenish yellow discharge, which adheres to the labia majora and dries upon them in yellow crusts. The children are, some of them, in perfect h ealth otherwise.

There is sometimes a history of pain upon urination or frequent micturition. There are no buboes, as a rule, but in many cases the inguinal glands may be very slightly enlarged. An examination shows the urethral orifice swollen and reddened, the seat of purulent exsudate, the hymen is much swollen and bathed in pus ; there may be erosions. When the patient cries, or if the perineum be pressed upward, a drop of pus exsudes from the vagina. If a Tuttle's urethral speculum be passed into the vagina and light thrown into the same by means of a head mirror, it is seen to be the seat of an intense inflammation. Like the vagina of the adult female in gonorrhœa it may be the seat of erosions which easily bleed. The cervix uteri is reddened and bathed in pus, and in the opening of the cervix we find a drop of pus. This cervical involvement I have seen in all the cases I have examined in this way. The pus when examined, either from the vagina or urethra, shows an immense number of leucocytes filled with diplococci which answer in form, size, grouping and stain reaction to the same forms seen in gonorrhœa of the urethra of the adult male. The course of the disease is tedious, and resists most methods of treatment. In many of these cases we have, as in the adult, joint complications and blenorrhagic conjunctivitis.

Etiology.—Most authors who have worked upon the etiology of vulvo-vaginitis in children have been struck by the constant presence of leucocytes in the discharge which are filled with micro-organisms, corresponding in size, form, grouping and stain to what is found in the discharge from the male urethra in true gonorrhœa. The question now is what significance can be attributed to these appearances. I need only briefly refer here to the discovery of a coccus or diplococcus in 1879 by Neisser, its thorough investigation by Bumm with its isolation and tests of virulence by the same author. The attacks of conscientious critics, no doubt, have been directed toward proving the negative value of these researches, so that lately, 1889, Neisser and his pupil, Steinschneider, have taken up the subject of the etiology of gonorrhœa anew. The articles of Neisser and Steinschneider owe their origin principally to the appearance of late of the work of Lustgarten and Manneberg upon the micro-organisms of the normal urethra. The authors last named showed the presence in the normal urethra in addition to other micro-organisms of diplococci which are in form and size so much like those of Neisser, that they asserted, should inflammation occur, they could invade leucocytes and be easily mistaken for them. They failed, however, to show any real examples of this error in diagnosis and all the mass of critique and matters published subsequently to this paper on the liability of error fails to show how these diplococci of the normal urethra actually were mistaken in certain cases for the real gonococci. Even Bockhard, who published a few cases of non-specific urethritis, failed to show that leucocytes might be crowded with this diplococcus in the manner seen in the gonorrhœal pus. Neisser naturally was again put upon the defensive, and anyone who will study his and Steinschneider's article will admit that both these authors make out a very good case for their gonococcus. To sum up the paper of Neisser in 1889, he says the non-gonorrhœal urethritis of the male is of so infrequent occurrence as to be practically of little importance diagnostically. The form, size, mode of arrangement against each other in pairs, and lastly, the grouping of these pairs in single large masses in cells, the peculiarity of stain by Gram (Roux); the isolation in exceptional cases if demanded by culture, and their capability of producing gonorrhœa when inoculated on the healthy urethra, all tend to show a specific micro-organism. The inoculation tends to prove the etiological connection. He lays stress upon the fact that chronic gonorrhœa, which is contagious, is so by virtue of the gonococcus. The vulvo-vaginitis in small girls, he thinks, is gonorrhœal. In the adult woman, he doubts the existence of gonorrhœa of the vagina and lays the existence of the disease in the urethra and cervix. All this with the evident conclusion that after examination of thousands of cases he has come to rely even on microscopic examination of a specimen of pus as to its gonorrhœal nature must convince the greatest skeptic. Steinschneider also went over the ground elaborated by Lustgarten and Manneberg and found five varieties of diplococci in the normal urethra. He found these so-called or rather *erroneously* called pseudo-gonococci in acute and chronic gonorrhœa, but concludes that in 95 per cent. of the cases the Roux stain gives absolutely reliable results. In 4.6 per cent. other diplococci than Neisser's decolorize. I think most workers who have stained much pus will be inclined to side with Neisser when he says that in skilled and tutored hands a mistake of identity is not possible. Lustgarten and Manneberg picture their normal diplococci on epithelial cells and not in leucocytes. I will show also these pseudo-gonococci upon epithelial cells in *vaginal discharge* of two cases of *simple catarrhal* non-gonorrhœal urogenital catarrh of young children.

yet it would be difficult to mistake them for gonococci. Turning now to vulvo-vaginal catarrh or urogenital blenorrhœa (Cahen-Brach) of young children and girls, it first struck Pott von Dusch, Spaeth that the cells, leucocytes, in the pus of these cases was identical with those found in gonorrhœa of the adult male. Since then this pus has been examined by Neisser,

FIG. 1.

SIMPLE VAGINITIS WITH PSEUDO-
GONOCOCCI ON EPITHELIAL CELLS.

FIG. 2.

SIMPLE VAGINITIS SHOWING
RODS, COCCI AND DIPLO-
COCCI IN LEUCOCYTES.

Steinschneider (four girls) Widmark, Ollivier, Hirschberg (blenorrhœa and vulvo-vaginitis), Fraenkel, Lober, Kratter, Epstein, Parrot, Deutschman, Martin, Comby, Cseri and myself, all with the uniform presence in the discharge from the vagina and urethra of leucocytes which contain diplococci answering

1   2

FIG. 3.

SCHEMATIC DRAWING TO ILLUSTRATE FORMS.

1. Group of pure serum culture diplococci of the normal vagina.
2. Group of diplococci from simple vaginitis, pure potato culture.

in every way to the descriptions of the diplococcus of Neisser. No author has, as yet, to my knowledge, made any attempts to cultivate the gonococcus Neisser, from the vaginal or urethral discharge of these children suffering from gonorrhœal vulvovaginitis. Steinschneider has only examined the pus microscopically, as also Epstein and Cahen-Brach. I have made

several attempts, I think, interesting ones, to isolate the gonococcus Neisser from the discharge in children, and beg to direct
attention only to the *diplococci* in the *normal vagina* of children and also the *abnormal* condition, which are apt to be mistaken for the gonococcus. In the *normal vagina* of the female
child we have a diplococcus which, when stained, resembles
closely the pseudo-gonococcus pictured by Lustgarten. It
grows upon blood serum in a whitish layer in small, white,
beaded colonies. In agar the surface growth is a whitish moist
layer and in puncture of gelatin tube there is a white non-characteristic growth. In colonies upon gelatin we have small,
round, granular, olive colored by transmitted and yellow-white
by reflected light. Some colonies of these diplococci are su
perficial and golden-yellow by *transmitted* light, whitish by
reflected light. It will thus be seen that it might be called a
diplococcus albus, and is stained and retains stains by Gram.
Turning our attention to the catarrhs of the vagina in children,
we have a *diplococcus* which I have found existing alone and in
almost pure culture in two cases of non-specific non gonorrhœal
vulvo-vaginitis. This vulvo-vaginitis, as I have cited in the
early part of this paper, is infectious, though not gonorrhœal ; see Cases IV. and V. (simple). This diplococcus does
not decolorize by Gram, it is about the size of the gonococcus. Sometimes it appears slightly larger or smaller. In
gelatin we find it grows in superficial and deep light straw
colored colonies, whitish by reflected light. The puncture inoculation in tubes is a whitish nail-like formation which, after
a time, fluidifies the gelatin slowly. In agar plates the colonies
are not characteristic. They are oval, deep or superficial,
round and spreading, the deep have a projection on one side.
On the surface of agar the growth is enamel white, moist
layer, no tendency to luxuriant spreading. In bouillon it
causes a general turbidity after twenty-four hours, and after
a few days a membrane forms on the surface of the bouillon.
On potato we find a luxuriant white creamy layer, moist,
raised, no great tendency to spread at sides. In appearance it
looks identical with the pseudo-gonococcus pictured by Lustgarten and Manneberg, and in my own cases was seen an epithelium of the vagina. The cases in which it was present will be
referred to again. The above diplococcus is also a white diplococcus.

A *third diplococcus* is a micro-organism which I think has,
with its fellow, a yellow diplococcus, been mistaken by many

enthusiasts for the gonococcus Neisser and so published. It is always in vulvo-vaginitis to be found in the discharges and grows so luxuriantly that I think it has been the principal agent in baffling my attempts at least to completely isolate the true Neisser coccus. This diplococcus is almost the exact counterpart in form to the true gonococcus. The first diplococcus is white, another is yellow and corresponds to what Bumm has described as the diplococcus flavus. These two diplococci I have isolated from gonorrhœal vulvo-vaginitis. The white diplococcus grows upon potato in a creamy layer almost indentical with the pseudo-gonococcus previously described. This creamy layer has a moist appearance, no tendency to spread at the sides. On agar this diplococcus grows in a pearly white layer and the stick in agar is not characteristic. It grows also in gelatin in a whitish non-characteristic stick—fluidifying the same slowly from the top. The yellow diplococcus grows, according to my notes on agar in form of a raised growth with wavy edges at first white and subsequently turning yellow in tint.

I have not used human serum in my attempts to isolate the gonococcus, not having even to-day any free access to human material, but the cow's serum was used, and it is well-known that the diplococcus Neisser grows sparingly on this medium and not as well as upon the serum and agar of Hueppe or human serum. It is not surprising that I only obtained what I think were very restricted gonococcus growths. If we inoculate drops of pus of a vulvo-vaginitis, according to Bumm's method, upon cow's serum, we find after twenty-four hours a fluidification of the serum, a sinking of the area of inoculation into the serum. In these excavations of serum tubes a diplococcus is found which is the exact counterpart of that seen in the crude pus sewn in tubes. If a needle is introduced into these excavations a thin, adhesive tenacious material can be extracted, and in this we find the diplococci mixed with other micro-organisms. By transferring several excavations contents to several tubes we sometimes are fortunate in obtaining a growth in yellow, white or creamy white layer on the serum composed of diplococci most of which *decolorize* with *Gram.* Not having used the plate method of agar serum of Hueppe (Werthheim), these growths were not pure gonococci, and in a few days, generally the fourth serum tube, they were outgrown by the diplococci last described above and lost. The remaining tubes showed diplococci which grew upon agar and gelatin and what was more discouraging did not decolorize with

Gram. These attempts at culture were begun as I stated, in intervals of other work as far back as 1889. This past two years I have again attempted their isolation always using bullock's serum, the result was the same. I think I can say that I had before me the gonococcus upon serum for it decolorized by Gram, but I could not hold it because it was contaminated by the rapidly growing diplococci always growing with it which I think are not specific. I did not use the methods so successfully adopted by Werthheim lately, but none the less it appears to me I would still have greatest difficulty in isolation and selection from this pseudo-diplococcus. Authors and workers have grown so skeptical to-day that if what is true as stated by Werthheim (which Bumm and Neisser do not agree to), that the gonococcus grows upon agar simple and mixed with human or cow's or sheep's serum, only inoculation experiments will in the future convince the critical reviewer that the coccus isolated from any case was the true Neisser coccus and not a pseudo variety. This discouraging outlook, for I could not persuade myself to try such inoculation for simple verification sake, has deterred me from further attempting the more complete isolation of the Neisser micro-organism from urogenital discharges of a gonorrhœal nature in children, while the apparent luxuriance of growth of the above *pseudo-gonococci* is an astonishing result of culture attempts and the difficulty of isolation of the true micro-organism responsible for the affections of the genito urinary tract of a gonorrhœal nature in children has baffled many observers notably Fraenkel. There can be no doubt of its active part in the etiology. Fraenkel has been successful in certain inoculations and lately Werthheim has been able to isolate the gonococcus in female subjects suffering with affections of the tubes and cause gonorrhœa in the male with pure culture. The various diplococci other than those isolated by myself, have in other hands proved non-pathogenic and incapable of producing gonorrhœa. Epstein attempted inoculation of gonorrhœal pus from his cases upon healthy children with negative results, and concludes from this that there must be peculiar conditions present of the mucous membrane to favor inoculation. To recapitulate in children we find *diplococci* in the normal vagina, in the simple catarrhal forms of urogenital blenorrhœa and lastly in the gonorrhœal forms of urogenital blenorrhœa.

1. Normal vagina, a white diplococcus not decolorized by Gram.

2. Simple catarrhal vulvo-vaginitis, a white diplococcus not decolorized by Gram.

Gonorrhœal vulvo-vaginitis.

3. White diplococcus, not decolorized by Gram.

4. Yellow diplococcus (diplococcus flavus Bumm).

All the above diplococci have a form and size apt to be mistaken for true Neisser diplococci, but in the material of over two hundred cases I have not met any case in which these so-called pseudo-diplococci existed in lucocytes alone exactly in the arrangement and disposition of true gonococci. They are found as a rule in pairs of two or four at most, in company with baccilli and simple micrococci or with streptococci in the leucocyte. In a small proportion of cases we find that long exposure of the crude pus spread on cover glass to the Gram method may even decolorize these diplococci as found also in the adult by Steinschneider, but the arrangement and disposition is so different from the true micro-organism as to guard against erroneous conclusions. The modes of staining these micro-organisms has given some workers difficulty, notably Fraenkel. The method pursued by the writer consisted in overstaining with gentian violet in anilin solution, decolorizing with alcohol lightly to find the presence of the coccus and reserving several glasses for Gram stain. At the same time to give good pictures the most satisfactory method has been to spread the pus thinly on cover glasses, heat for some little time on the Ehrlich plate below the 100° C point ; after complete drying stain first with a dilute aqueous solution of crystalized eosin and then wash and transfer to a dilute solution in water of Loeffler's menthyl blue alkaline solution. Beautiful pictures can thus be obtained. If stained first with blue and then eosin, the eosin is apt to decolorize the blue stained diplococci, giving very erroneous pictures. I have mentioned these points, having worked them out in many cases. Baumgarten's method of staining intensely with methyl violet and slightly decolorizing with alcohol, also gives good results. I have not tried safranine being so well pleased with the blue and eosin stain. The Gram stain is the differential stain only, and pictures obtained with gentian anilin solution are apt to be overstained and confused. I have obtained with the eosin-blue stain beautiful pictures of the eosinophile leucocytes mentioned by Ehrlich as evidence that we here deal with leucocytes directly emigrated from the blood vessels. Ehrlich has found these leucocytes in cases of gonorrhœa in the adult. I obtained them in my cases of gonorrhœal urethritis of boys, also in simple and gonorrhœal vulvo-vaginitis. They are simply diagnostic of the truth maintained by Ehrlich, that the eosinophile cells are not artifacts. I have elaborated the simple stain methods in order that others may be aided thereby. *Measurements.* The measurements of the *true gonococcus* are 0.8μ to 1.6μ (micro-millimeters) in the long diameter, average 1.25μ and 0.6 to 0.8μ in the line of the interspace.

The *pseudo-gonococci* found in the normal vagina of the child measure 0.8 to 1.24μ (micro-millimeters) in the long diameter, and have a breadth of 0.8μ in the interspace.

The *pseudo-gonococci* found by me in cases of simpler uro-genital blenorrhœa, have a diameter of 0.9μ (micro-millimeters) to 1.28μ (micro-millimeters) in long diameter, and 0.9μ (micro-millimeters) in breadth at the interspace.

The *pseudo-gonococci* found by me in the gonorrhœas of female children measure 1.24μ (micro-millimeters) to 0.9μ (micro-millimeters) long diameter, and in the interspace the same as the previous pseudo-gonococci.

It will be seen as above, that all these diplococci, when care-fully measured, are not only much the same size, but all the measurements are for practical purposes, identical with those of the true gonococcus. It will be also noted that in growth the pseudo-gonococci act much the same in artificial media, and it would be difficult to diagnose them apart from their particular form of disease.

Urethritis in boys and young children.—1. There is a sim-ple non-specific inflammation of the meatus urinarius in male children, which is manifested by an eroded condition of the meatus. The child suffers in passing water, because the slight secretion of pus dries on the orifice of the glans penis, and pre-vents the passage of urine. The urine, when voided, also causes pain. In some cases the meatus alone is eroded, in others, if the glans is pressed, a small drop of pus can be expressed from the anterior part of the urethra. This condition, which might be called simple erosion of the meatus and catarrh of the fossa navicularis, is obscure in its origin. I have often thought it might be caused by an infection in children who crawl about on the ground and thus get filth over the organ, infection being favored by a slight scratch or wound. I confess, however, that this is unsatisfactory, as it has occurred to me to see this condi-tion in babes who cannot crawl about alone. It must be caused by some unnatural interference with the parts by nurses or par-ents, though not, however, with bad intent.

I have often examined the drop of pus in the cases of simple anterior urethritis, and never found anything but what is found in simple catarrhal processes. Nothing characteristic of gonorrhœa was ever found by me.

2. True gonorrhœa has occurred in a number of male children in my service, and some of the children quite young, one a baby in arms. The symptoms of urethritis in male children give much the picture seen in the adult male, with the exception that the constitutional disturbances are almost nil. Rona has lately recorded some fifteen cases of gonorrhœa in boys of various ages. He has never observed orchitis in any of his cases, but has had balanoposthitis and severe lymphadenitis or even lymphangoitis as complications. In a baby 15 months old, there was severe epididymitis of both sides, of weeks' duration. Rona has seen a case of real stricture of the urethra in a boy 11 years old. Bokai has seen some cases of true gonorrhœa in boys, but has never seen a stricture. It may be mentioned here that the cases of my first group, though not complete and typical urethritis, do not find their counterpart in the adult, at least not frequently. Within the past six months alone I have seen three cases of true gonorrhœa in boys 3 years, 6½ years, and 9 years old respectively. The histories of the cases are much the same. The boys in the primary stage had much swelling of the body and glans of the penis. There was a profuse, thick green discharge from the urethra, frequent micturition, and very little pain complained of. In one case I was able to watch until no discharge, not even serous discharge was apparent. This boy, I think, was really cured ; it is now a month, and he has not returned. The disease ran its course—a very mild one—in about seven weeks. The other boys disappeared from observation. In 1889, I saw a baby, 18 months old, with the same symptoms. Here, also, swelling of the glans was severe, and the baby seemed to suffer very much.

The etiology of the cases in two of the boys is interesting as tending to prove in an almost absolutely conclusive clinical way that the vulvo-vaginitis gonorrhœica of girls is really such and capable of causing urethritis in the male. These two boys æt 5 and 9 years, had attempted intercourse with a small girl living in the same tenement. They sent the girl to me and the girl (case III gon.), was suffering from a vulvo-vaginitis which was gonorrhœal. It would be difficult, I think, to find three more convincing cases in the literature of contagion. They go also to prove Epstein's supposition to be correct that peculiar condi-

tions of the sexual concours favors contagion, for, as stated, his
inoculations from gonorrhœal babies to the urethræ of babies
were negative.

Examination of the pus of *non-gonorrhœal* cases of anterior
urethritis gives pus cells which are the seat of isolated diplococcus forms, but in no way resembling gonococci, proving that
in the male urethra in children as in the adult there are also so-
called pseudo-gonococci.

Examination of pus of the gonorrhœal cases in boys and
babies gives true diplococcus (Neisser) pictures in all their ex-
quisite and absolutely convincing detail of form, arrangement
in groups and masses filling up the leucocytes, size, reaction to
stain tests. I have also in these cases found the leucocytes
filled with eosinophile granulations. The methods of stain were
as detailed with the female children.

Mode of Infection.—The theories of Pott and others who
wrote upon the gonorrhœal form of urogenital blenorrhœa
(vulvo-vaginitis), in young children presupposed that many of
these cases originated in an indirect way from the use of utensils
by the children in families whose adults were the sufferers from
gonorrhœa, male or female. There are, of course, examples of
gonorrhœa being conveyed to children in this indirect way but
this does not account for a large proportion of cases. In my
own experience I have never treated cases which could be legally
construed as those in which children had been dealt with by
adults in a forcible manner and thereby contracted gonorrhœa.
These cases are all carefully weeded out of my service and referred to the surgeons in charge of the police precinct station.
They are of no interest to the author of this paper. But the
great mass of my cases are true gonorrhœas and those in which
the origin has been kept secret very skilfully by parents, children or both. I believe many of them originate in actual sexual
contact either accidental or with intent. This may occur acci-
dentally among the poor where, as in case, XIII, there was
a history of a man sleeping in the same bed with the child. The
mother protested though not even questioned, that the man was
not to blame. It was probably some one nearer than a stranger to
the child. In another case (IX. gonorrhœal), the mother told
me in great distraction that she had slept with the child. Had
been ill for weeks with a discharge. Examination of the mother
showed salpingo-oöphoritis with also urethritis and endocervicitis. In the urethra of the mother I found gonococci. In
another acute case in a child I obtained the same history but

though the mother had a discharge (urethritis and vaginitis and endocervicitis), I did not find gonococci. Her discharge was six months old and it may, as Neisser has pointed out in these cases, have required repeated examinations to find the gonococcus. I have spoken of the mode of infection in two of the boys. In the third case of a boy the gonorrhœa was contracted from an older boy with whom he had had relations.

I have also shown, I think, conclusively, that the simple catarrhal vulvo-vaginitis is an entity as real as the gonorrhœal form. How do they originate in face of the fact that in the male simple typical urethritis is so great a rarity (Neisser Bockhardt)? I think in girls everything is favorable to infection. The parts are not protected as the male urethra is. The mucous membrane is peculiarly favorable to reaction under irritants. The mothers are constantly interfering with these parts in children. In the exanthemata the vagina and vulva react as does any other organ, the nose, ear, glans, etc., to mixed infections. But where no history of exanthemata exists, the tracing of infection is difficult. Among the poor the herding together of parents and children in the same bed may favor contagion from the mothers who suffer from simple vaginitis. I have shown that the simple vulvo-vaginitis in children is contagious also. I have purposely recorded a case in my collection of gonorrhœal ophthalmia in a child of very mild type in which the swelling and chemosis of the conjunctiva was not so extreme. One eye only was affected, gonococci were found in the pus. I had treated the mother before the delivery of this babe for what I thought was gonorrhœal disease of the genitals. This child recovered with simple cloudiness of the cornea. I have simply noted this case in order to point out modes of contagion Epstein does not believe in indirect contagion and Parrot has also come to the conclusion that contagion from clothes, towels, sheets of the mother is difficult if possible. He has never seen a vulvo-vaginitis result from a gonorrhœal conjunctivitis. I have noted a case in which I think pustular eczema of the labia majora caused simple catarrh of the urethra and vagina and also suppurating inguinal bubo (III. of simple).

In case VII. of the simple forms I have not the slightest doubt that the simple vaginitis of the mother caused the disease. The pus may have been conveyed from the fingers of the mother to the parts of the infant.

The seat of disease. In vulvo-vaginal catarrh, simple and gonorrhœal, most authors, even recent writers (Cahen-Brach) are inclined to place the primary infection in vulvo-vaginal catarrh in the urethra, and look upon the infection of the hymen, vagina and cervix uteri as secondary. However this may be, I have never seen in all my large material a case in which I could say that the urethra alone was affected. When the cases come to me the urethra, hymen and vagina are found all the seat of disease in all forms of intensity in both simple and gonorrhœal cases with the exception of case VII of simple form. Neisser and Bumm, believe that the vagina in children can be the seat of gonorrhœal disease, whereas in adults, as is well known, they still believe gonorrhœal vaginitis is not an actuality. Werthheim's work, if it is further corroborated, will tend to explode the old theory that the gonococcus can only flourish upon columnar epithelial surfaces. Werthheim showed that not only the peritoneum could be invaded by the gonococcus solely and purely, but that the planes of connective tissues could be subject to invasion and this in actual inoculation experiments. Thus many infections formerly thought to be due to mixed infections, will come under the heading of true gonorrhœal diseases caused by the gonococcus wholly. The cases of vulvo-vaginitis which I have seen, have, if gonococci were present, yielded this abundantly in the discharge of pus from the *vagina* as well as that of the urethra obtained directly by first cleaning the parts and then squeezing a drop of pus from this tube. In those cases in which the urethral pus was examined, the gonococci cells were not so numerous, though a purer secretion of gonococci exists in the urethra. I have come to believe that the urethra, nymphæ and hymen, the vagina and uterine cervical canal are all the seat of gonorrhœal disease, and one of the chief causes of the intractible nature of the various forms of vulvo-vaginitis is the fact of the involvement of the vagina and cervix, the latter especially difficult to treat in small children. I know that Cahen-Brach intimates that infection of the vagina by urethral pus can be avoided by means of tamponade. Infection of these parts spreads rapidly, and when we see them, at least in my own material, the mischief to the vagina has been done and seems to play a leading rôle.

This is proven in most cases very distinctly by making the vagina the point of attack in treatment. If this is done as will be detailed, the symptoms rapidly subside quicker than by any means known to the author. The irrigation and local treatment of the vagina results in most acute cases in a rapid diminution in the amount and change in character of the discharge.

Even those cases in which Cahen-Brach said he prevented infection of the vagina (and no doubt he did prevent marked disease of this tube) it will be noticed he. always, at each sitting, irrigated the vagina with sublimate before tamponading the same, preparatory to treatment of the urethra.

In simple urogenital blenorrhœa we may have the vagina affected without the urethra being in the remotest way diseased. This is shown in case VII of the simple group where I do not doubt the infection was conveyed from a simple vaginitis of the mother to the infant in some way. In this case I took great pains to examine the urethra of the child by scraping the secretion in the long diameter out of the tube, no leucocytes were found and only isolated bacterial forms, while the vagina was markedly inflammed. The broad expanse of mucous membrane presented by the vagina and hymen as compared to the urethra would naturally prepare one for more disturbance here, and also a more convenient place for infection than the urethra. Thus far my studies convince me that in both forms of urogenital blenorrhœa the vaginal process plays as much a rôle as that of the urethra. I grant, however, that my studies have convinced me that the urethral mucous membrane is a more favorable abiding place for the gonococcus. Even in children (vide case wherein gonococci existed after six months). In the vagina the gonorrhœal process, after a time, in old cases, is replaced by a species of desquamative catarrh in which all traces of gonorrhœal diagnostic elements may be obliterated or scanty in number and difficult to find.

Complications.—The only complication which I have had any experience with and of which I shall treat, are in the female children, ophthalmia, arthritis and bubo. Ophthalmia is a much more frequent complication in children than in the adult. I have observed it in the gonorrhœal cases alone, and in 1890 published such a case in a child three years old, in the *New York Medical Journal*. The blenorrhœa affected both eyes ; in this patient there was also the complication of arthritis. It has been asserted that the eye of the child is especially susceptible to contagion, hence the frequency with which we meet blenorrhœa in these children. The cases of blenorrhœa which I have had, showed the same leucocytes filled with gonococci in the pus of the eye as in that of the vaginal discharge. In 1890 I published two cases of arthritis complicating gonorrhœal urogenital blenorrhœa in young girls. In both these cases I have found

the gonococcus in the vaginal discharge and published microphoto-
graphs of the same. Hartley in 1887, *New York Medical Journal*,
also published some cases similar to these. Deutschman, an oph-
thalmologist, observed arthritis in children suffering from gonorrhœal ophthalmia ; he found what he thought was the gonococcus in the joint effusions. Petrone, Kammerer and Hartley
publish cases in which they have found what they accept as the
gonococcus in joint effusions. Brieger and Ehrlich, on the other
hand, are equally confident in asserting their non-existence and
attributing the joint affections complicating gonorrhœa, as due
to a so called mixed infection. However this may be, we see
that in these small children the joints are liable to react in much
the same way as in the adult gonorrhœal cases. Brieger, Ehrlich, Baumgarten, Sanger doubt the presence of the gonococcus
in the blood, lymph channels or in joint effusions. Werthheim,
however, contends, as already stated, that the gonococcus can
invade the lymph channels. Thus the isolated cases of periton-
itis, joint affection, endocarditis would be regarded from such
a standpoint as really caused by the gonococcus. These points
remain still to be more fully studied. The joints which I have
seen most frequently affected have been the knee joint, the an-
kle, the wrist joint. I have not as yet seen cases of involvement of the very small joints. This, perhaps, is a matter of detail. Gerhardt has published cases of gonorrhœal arthritis in
older girls above eighteen years of age. I refer to the article
on arthritis complicating vulvo-vaginal inflammation in children
by me for more detailed literature.

Relapsing cases, and the presence of gonococci in old cases.
—The author has found the gonococcus persist in cases of
vulvo-vaginitis in girls, after eight weeks, or nine weeks, or six
months (case XVII). In these cases the cells containing the typical pictures of gonococci will be found to be very few. The pus
in these cases should be collected from the urethra or deep vaginal fornix. In old cases it should be a routine to examine pus
from the urethra or vaginal fornix repeatedly for gonococci, if
we are in any way desirous of fixing an exact diagnosis. Neisser has called especial attention to this in the adult and in
children it holds good that a discharge may be pronounced
simple which is really gonorrhœal, especially in old cases, if
fortune and perseverance does not favor in discovering the few
leucocytes with typical gonococci.

There is also a distinct class of cases which should always be
looked upon with suspicion. These are the relapsing urogenital

blenorrhœas. The history obtained in these cases is that the child has suffered for months from a discharge which had ceased being thought cured. In a few weeks or months such a discharge will reappear. Many of these cases are gonorrhœal. Neisser has dilated upon such a class of cases in adults, and in children we have their distinct counterparts. The gonococcus nested in the myriads of rugæ and asperities of the female-urogenital tract will apparently lie dormant to regain energy and cause renewed symptoms at favorable moments. Sparse discharges of recurrent cases should be repeatedly examined, if possible, to find the gonococcus. More especially so, if there is a history of conveyance of the disease from one child to another. Among the cases of old gonorrhœa, I refer the reader to case XVII. (gonorrhœal), especially where for the past six months previous to visit, the child had a discharge, which at first profuse, was finally very spare. At first examination it seemed it might be simple catarrh, but subsequent careful search in the minutest quantity of urethral pus revealed diplococci (Neisser.)

Treatment.—In order not to repeat the literature upon treatment, I will simply say that all the new methods recommended for the treatment of this affection, thalin, iodoform bougies, injections, silver applications, have been used by me with the same degree of success as that obtained by others. They have failed to effect what we may call a shortening of the disease. The discharge ceases, under the above treatment, to be profuse, but the patients complain that small amounts of secretion are found on the vulva every morning. The disease drags on a course of six, eight, or even twelve weeks. Being convinced that this prolonged discharge from the parts is in part aided by the anatomical nature of the vagina and cervix uteri, I have adopted the following course in all cases.

The parts being cleansed with 1-5000 sublimate, externally, a Tuttle's urethral speculum is introduced into the vagina, and the same is thoroughly douched with sublimate, 1-5000. The parts are then dried with a uterine applicator and cotton, and a 10 per cent. solution of nitrate of silver is carried upon a cotton applicator into the vagina up to the cervix, and the parts thoroughly painted with the same. The vagina is again douched with 1-5000 sublimate, and the speculum withdrawn. In acute cases the applications cause some bleeding, due to erosions in the vagina ; this soon ceases after a few applications, and further treatment.is not attended with any stains of blood on the applicators. The silver is at first applied daily, and then every other day. Under this treatment the discharge ceases to be profuse within a few days, but I am not in a position to give exact data. I can recommend it as being the most satisfactory mode of treatment, and the most rational method to employ. The children struggle with every mode of treatment, but with good table and appliances, less harm is done by the above modes than by simply trying to introduce bougies, which give pain and cause no end of trouble. I have refrained, in all my cases, from treating the urethra of girls. The parts are so small that the pain resulting from interference with the urethra by our present methods does not justify persistence in efforts of treatment. The eye and joint complications I generally have referred to the surgeon for treatment The bubo presents nothing peculiar.

ILLUSTRATIVE CASES.

I. *Simple non-gonorrhœal urogenital blenorrhœal vulvo-vaginitis.*—L. G., aged 6 years, suffering for the past four weeks from a vaginal and urethral discharge. The discharge from the urethra shows only isolated diplococci not characteristic of gonorrhœa.

II. *Simple relapsing form.*—S. H., aged 6 years, has three months ago had a discharge from the vagina. It had apparently ceased and now has returned. The vagina shows a gleety yellow discharge, slight redness of the nymphæ, no gonococci in urethral or vaginal secretion.

III. Simple form with *bubo.*—Ida L., aged 5 years, has had a discharge from the vulva now of twenty-four hours' duration. On the vulva there are pustules and in the introitus aphthous ulcerations. The vagina and urethra show a purulent discharge and there is an impetigo upon the vulva (labia majora.) The vaginal discharge is green and thin. The right inguinal lymph nodes suppurating.

Examination of urethral and vaginal discharge shows no gonococci. Two cases of non-gonorrhœal discharge repeatedly examined and nothing found but pseudo-gonococci which were also isolated and cultivated.

IV. R. M., aged 7 years, has for past two weeks suffered from a yellow discharge, no urinary symptoms, no redness of parts. This child has had a discharge a year ago.

Pus from vagina and urethra shows pure examples of pseudo-gonococci. (Lustgarten.)

V. Annie M., sister to above, suffers from a urogenital blenorrhœa, two weeks duration. The discharge is not great but whitish, purulent, no urinary symptoms, no redness of parts.

Repeated examination of urethral and vaginal pus shows the above pseudo-gonococci.

VI. Healthy child 3½ years old has been sick a week with painful and frequent micturition. Mother has noticed that mornings the child has discharge from the vulva adherent in crusts, not abundant. Parts are swollen but not markedly so. Discharge is greenish yellow fluid and just moistens the parts. The urethral orifice bathed with drop of pus. Nymphæ swollen and tender. Child has slept with mother who has a babe eight weeks old. Urethral and vaginal pus carefully and separately examined ; no characteristic gonococci. The bacilli, and pseudo-diplococci (as in V and VI cases), did not decolorize with Gram.

· VII. *Simple non-gonorrhœal vaginitis without any signs of urethritis.*—S. G., infant aged 12 months well nourished. Has for the past week shown a discharge from the genitals   There are no other symptoms. Examination shows that the vulva is of normal hue, not eroded, no crusts or discharge visible, urethra also perfectly normal but the hymen is somewhat swollen but not reddened in hue. The orifice is bathed in pus ; squeezing the perineum causes the appearance at the hymenal orifice of a thick viscid creamy yellow discharge. Child sleeps with its mother. The mother is six months pregnant but examination shows nothing abnormal. The leucorrhœa of mother is normal in quantity and what we would expect in a woman at this period.

The pus of vagina of child was examined but absolutely nothing found but pure pus, in a few of the leucocytes isolated single pseudo-diplococci, these even were rare. The infant's urethra was scraped but absolutely no pus cells were obtained showing it was not inflamed.

The mother's urethra examined, no leucocytes indicating inflammation present, only epithelium, pseudo-diplococci and other bacteria.

I. *Gonorrhœal vulvo-vaginitis or urogenital blenorrhœa.*— L. R. aged 4 years. Mother has noticed discharge for the past two days from vulva. Patient complains of pain on passing urine and when walking. She has yellow crusts of dried pus on labia majora, a thick greenish yellow discharge from the vagina. The nymphæ are much swollen as also hymenal structure. Hymen imperforate, meatus urinarius red and swollen.

Pus contains gonococci.

II. S. F. aged 4 years. The discharge from vagina thick and greenish hue, has yellowish crusts on labia majora, has been ill six days. Has been in a leading hospital for tubercular disease of jaw and returned home with the discharge.

Pus shows gonococci.

III. C. S., girl who has communicated gonorrhœa to two boys. Examined in the seventh week of the disease. There is a urethral and vaginal discharge and the vulva is reddened and eroded.

1

The discharge is spare and gleety ; when examined very characteristic gonococci found.

IV. S. D., aged 2 years. For past three days there has been a thick yellowish green discharge from vulva. Discharge is abundant about the urethra and dries upon the labia majora in crusts.

Pus contains abundant gonococci.

V. C. M., aged 10 years. Pale and anæmic child has had a thick greenish yellow discharge from genitals for the past eight days, no other history, denies symptoms of any kind.

Pus examined, gonococci.

VI. Jenny S., aged 3½ years, has for the past six days suffered from a discharge from the genitals, which is thick, greenish and dries in crusts upon the labia majora. Parts are swollen and painful at the introitus, no inguinal adenitis.

Pus examined gives gonococci.

VII. D. R., 6 years old. Has for the past three days complained of painful and frequent micturition. She has had a thick yellow discharge from genitals which dries in crusts on the labia majora. There is great swelling of the nymphæ.

Gonococci in pus.

VIII. *Gonorrhœal vulvo-vaginitis with pains in the joints.* —M. W., sick with vaginal discharge for past two weeks. A week ago complained of pains in the ankles and the right wrist. The discharge is a profuse greenish one and the nymphæ and hymen are sensitive, swollen. Crusts on the vulva, no temperature, no bubo.

Discharge shows gonococci.

IX. F. B., aged 4 years. Four weeks before visit had measles. A week before consultation mother noticed a greenish yellow discharge on clothes. This has continued since. There have been no urinary symptoms. Child is intelligent and robust. There is erosion of vulva ; introitus and urethra painful and swollen, the discharge is thin and fluid. That from the vagina contains abundant gonococci. The mother of this child has, for the past three days, complained of painful and frequent micturition but secretion from urethra of mother shows nothing definite. Mother sleeps with child.

X. M. R., aged 6 years, has been in a leading metropolitan hospital. Six days before visit was discharged from the hospital when mother noticed the vaginal discharge. The discharge from the vagina dries in crusts on the labia majora, no symptoms referable to bladder. The labia majora are eroded, the vaginal and urethral discharge is thick and yellow, parts about the introitus inflammed and much swollen and painful.

· Pus from vagina contains gonococci which persisted after eight weeks, when patient returned to begin treatment anew. Then discharge very small in amount but a few gonococci present.

XI. C. H., 8 years old, has had a discharge for two weeks from the genitals. Has never had such an illness before. There are no urinary symptoms. The pus is white, creamy, and does not excoriate the labia. The child has slept with her mother who, for some time past has suffered from a profuse vaginal discharge, frequent and painful micturition. Mother's discharge is thick, ropy and yellow. Mother volunteered statement that child may have contracted the disease from her.

Examination. Pus of vagina of child shows abundant gonococci. The pus taken from urethra of mother contains a few leucocytes giving typical gonococcus pictures.

XII. A L , aged 4 years. has for a week been ill with a yellow discharge from the vagina and urethra. There is no history of urinary symptoms. The introitus vagina painful, red and somewhat swollen. Pus from the vagina showed gonococci.

XIII. A. G., aged 4 years. Two weeks ago the child had developed a discharge from the vagina, frequent, but no history of painful micturition. There has been some malaise, no buboes. Urethral opening, nymphæ and hymen all red, painful, swollen; pus taken from the vaginal opening contains abundant gonococci. The mother volunteered statement that child had slept in same bed with a man who she asserted was sick (?).

XIV. C. M., well nourished child aged 8 years, has for the past two weeks suffered from a purulent discharge from the genitals. There is frequent micturition but no marked pain ; no other history.

Examination shows erosions around introitus ; same is painful and swollen. The pus discharged from the urethra and vagina is thick and greenish in hue ; no enlarged inguinal glands.

Pus contains abundant gonococci.

XV. S. B. No previous history. Child is 5 years old and well nourished. The vaginal discharge is of one day's standing ; no other symptoms ; no buboes ; no pain on urination. The child sleeps with mother who for five months has suffered from a vaginal leucorrhœa.

Examination. Pus from child, gonococci.

Examination. Pus from mother, no gonococci. (Cervix and urethra examined.)

XVI. A. W., 5 years old. Has suffered for five days from a discharge from the genitals. No history of painful micturition or frequent desire to pass urine. Child is very robust and well built for its age. Has a very profuse discharge from the urethra and vagina, which show abundant gonococci.

XVII. Old gleety form in which urethra showed gonococci six months after onset of disease.

M. R., 6 years of age, has for the past six months had a

vaginal discharge which at times was profuse at others scanty. There has been burning pain upon passing urine. Introitus is red and spongy with a very scanty vaginal discharge of a thin consistence and greenish in hue. Urethral orifice swollen and reddened.

Pus taken from urethral canal shows gonococci.

I. *Simple erosions and catarrh of the anterior urethra in boys.*—Boy 9 years old suffers from an erosion or impetiginous condition of the meatus urinarius. By squeezing the glans a small drop of pus can be expressed from the urethra. This pus contains cells the seat of isolated diplococci, but they do not have the arrangement of gonococci. No other history as to origin of affection.

II. Boy aged 5 years. For the past week has had an ulcerated and sore condition of the meatus urinarius. When the glans penis is pressed a small drop of pus exsudes from the urethra.

Cover glasses show no gonococci.

I. *Gonorrhœal urethritis in boys.*—S. B. Intelligent boy aged 5 years, not abnormal in physique. Has for several days had a urethral discharge. Thick yellow. The glans, penis and body of penis much swollen. Makes statement that he has played with child in same house (history related elsewhere). This child was small girl 7 years old suffering from gonorrhœal urogenital blenorrhœa.

Pus from boy's urethra showed gonococci.

Case sent to me by Dr. W. W. Van Arsdale.

II. Boy aged 9 years came to me with a gleety, milky discharge from the urethra. Penis somewhat swollen, the boy has no other symptoms and denies that there is painful or frequent micturition. States he contracted the disease from same girl as case I.

III. P. B. Boy aged 6½ years, intelligent, robust, brought to me with a creamy white discharge from the urethra. There is much œdema of the glans, and penis and this condition said to have been worse. Is sick now fourteen days. States that another boy gave him the trouble (?). The boy cured apparently after 7 weeks of treatment. Urethral pus shows gonococci.

IV. A specimen in my collection, dated August 1889, taken from the urethra of a babe 18 months old, who, for two weeks, had an abundant discharge from urethra, the glans, penis and body of penis is much swollen, child is very restless and evinces signs of pain when organ is examined. No history. Pus of urethra contains gonococci.

LITERATURE. LEADING NOTICES ONLY.

1. Patt. *Jahrbuch. f. Kindheilk*, Bd., XIX, 1883, s. 7.
2. E. Fraenkel. *Virch. Archiv. Bd.*, 99, 1885, s. 251.

3. Widmark. *Archiv. f. Kind. Heilk.*, Bd., VII, s. 1.
4. Spaeth. *Miln. Med. Wochen.*, 1888.
5. Ollivier. *Le Concours Med.*, 1888, Nov. 3.
6. Bouchout. Treatise Diseases Children.
7. Hirschberg. *Berlin. Klin. Wochen.*, 1884.
8. Epstein. *Archiv. f. Dermatol. u. Syph.* Bd. 23, 1891
9. Lober. *La Semaine Med.* 1887.
10. Hartley. *N. Y. Med. Jour.*, 1887.
11. Kratter. *Berlin. Klin. Wochen.*, 1890, No. 42.
12. Vibert and Bordas. *La Médicine Moderne*, 1890, No. 47, 1891, No. 1.
13. Parrot. Jahrb. f. Kindheilk. Bd., XVIII, p. 346
14. Suchard. *Rev. Mens des. Enfance.*
15. Deutschman. *Archiv. f. Ophthalmol.*, 1890.
16. Werthheim. *Archiv. f. Gynæc.*, Bd. XLII, 1892.
17. Martin. *Jour. Cutaneous and Genito-Urinary Diseases*, Vol. X, No. 11.
18. Comby. *Rev. des Malad. des Enfance*, Jan. 1892.
19. Dusch. *Internat. Rundsch*, Wien II, 647.
20. Cséri. *Wien Med. Wochensch.*, XXXV, 703.
21. S. Loven. *Centralbl. f. Gynæc.* No. 10, 1887.
22. Neisser, A. Naturforscher Versammlung, Straasburg, 1889.
23. Giovanni. *Centralbl. f. Med. Wissen.*, 1886, No. 48.
24. Bockhard. *Monatsheft f. Prakt. Dermatologie*, Bd. V, 1886.
25. Steinschneider. Same as Neisser.
26. V. Dutsch. *Deutsch. Med. Wochenschr*, 1888. No. 41.
27. Touton. *Archiv. f. Dermatol. u. Syph.*, 1889.
28. P. Roux. *Archiv. f. Dermatol. u. Syph.* 1893.
29. Cahen-Brach. *Jahrb. f. Kindheilk.* Bd., XXXIV, hft. 4.
30. John A. Wyeth. *Kansas City Med. Index*, 1892.
31. H. Koplik. *N. Y. Med. Jour.*, 1890, June 21.
32. Sanger. Die Tripper ansteckung beim Weiblichen Geschlecht, Leipzig, 1889.
33. Lustgarten and Mannaberg. *Verteljahrschrift f. Derm.*, 1889.